LACROSSE

Don Wells

WEIGL PUBLISHERS INC.

Published by Weigl Publishers Inc.

350 5th Avenue, 59th Floor

New York, NY 10118

Library of Congress Cataloging-in-Publication Data

Wells, Donald.
  For the love of lacrosse / by Don Wells.
     p. cm. -- (For the love of sports)
  Includes index.
  ISBN 978-1-59036-297-6 (hard cover : alk. paper) -- ISBN 978-1-59036-301-0 (soft cover : alk. paper)
  1. Lacrosse--Juvenile literature. I. Title. II. Series.
  GV989.14.W45 2006
  796.347--dc22

                                    2004029148

Printed in the United States in North Mankato, Minnesota

4 5 6 7 8 9 14 13 12 11 10

092010

WEP08092010

Photograph credits
Cover: Long Island Lizards versus Rochester Rattlers, Major League Lacrosse (Al Bello/ALLSPORT/Getty Images)

Brock University: pages 3, 5L, 11, 14; **Getty Images:** pages 1 (Ezra Shaw/Allsport), 4 (Topical Press Agency), 5R (Al Bello/Allsport), 6 (Al Bello/Allsport), 7 (PhotoDisc Green), 8 (Doug Pensinger/Allsport), 10L (PhotoDisc Green), 10R (Doug Pensinger/Allsport), 12 (Doug Pensinger/Allsport), 13 (Al Bello/Allsport), 15T (Phil Masturzo/Time Life Pictures), 15B (Al Bello/Allsport), 16 (Doug Pensinger/Allsport), 17 (Neil Liefer/Time Inc./Time Life Pictures), 18L (David Maxwell), 18R (Kimberly Butler/Time Life Pictures), 19L (Kimberly Butler/Time Life Pictures), 20 (Stockbyte Gold), 21T (Phil Masturzo/Time Life Pictures), 21B (PhotoDisc Green), 22 (Orlando/Three Lions), 23 (Doug Pensinger/Allsport);
University of Maryland: page 19R.

Project Coordinator

Tina Schwartzenberger

Design

Warren Clark

Layout

Kathryn Livingstone

Substantive Editor

Frances Purslow

Photo Researcher

Kim Winiski

Contents

What is Lacrosse?

Lacrosse is North America's oldest team sport. During the 1600s, French **missionaries** in what is now Canada watched Native Americans play a game called *baggataway*. Baggataway was played to train warriors, settle disputes between tribes, and during ceremonies. The missionaries called the game *la crosse* because the head of the stick players used resembled the cross **bishops** carried.

Baggataway teams often had between 100 and 1,000 players. A large rock or tree was used as the goal. The two team's goals were usually 500 yards (457 meters) apart. Sometimes they were several miles apart. Players scored by hitting the goal with a ball or by hitting the ball between goal posts. Native-American lacrosse games could last 2 to 3 days.

Since 1903, Cambridge University and Oxford University, both in Great Britain, have played a yearly lacrosse match.

A Canadian dentist named W. George Beers introduced the first modern set of lacrosse rules. He determined the size of the playing field, the number of players on each team, and other basic rules.

More than 5,500 women play lacrosse at 240 American colleges and universities.

Lacrosse has been played in the United States since the 1880s. At that time, lacrosse was played mostly at colleges along the east coast of the United States. It has slowly grown in popularity across the country. Today, people in more than twenty countries play lacrosse. It is Canada's official summer game.

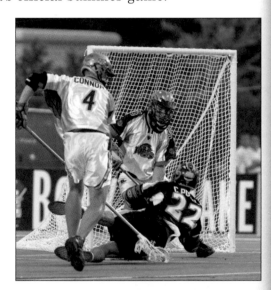

Professional outdoor lacrosse has been played in the United States since 2001.

CHECK IT OUT

Visit the Oneida Nation online to learn more about the history of lacrosse at **www.oneida-nation.net/ lacrosse.html**

Getting Ready to Play

Lacrosse can be a rough game. Players need special equipment to prevent injuries while playing lacrosse.

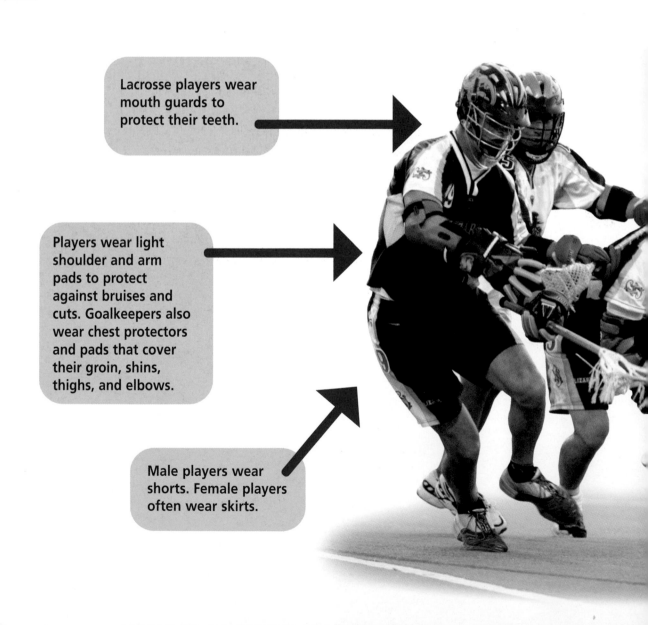

Lacrosse players wear mouth guards to protect their teeth.

Players wear light shoulder and arm pads to protect against bruises and cuts. Goalkeepers also wear chest protectors and pads that cover their groin, shins, thighs, and elbows.

Male players wear shorts. Female players often wear skirts.

The lacrosse ball is hard rubber. It measures about 2 inches (6 centimeters) across and weighs about 5 ounces (142 grams).

Each player uses a stick, or crosse, with a hook at the end that is crossed with cord to form a small net, or pocket. Players use the stick to catch, carry, and throw the ball. Only the goalkeeper can touch the ball with his or her hands.

Men wear helmets with face guards. The helmet and face guard protect players from face and head injuries.

Players wear jerseys in their team colors. Jerseys are loose to allow players to easily twist their bodies and swing their arms.

Players wear gloves to protect their hands.

Lacrosse players wear shoes with **cleats**. The shoes help players grip the ground and prevent slipping. When playing indoors on concrete, players wear sneakers.

The Field

Outdoor lacrosse is called field lacrosse. It is played on a rectangular grass field. Women usually play on a larger field than men. There is also an indoor version of lacrosse called box lacrosse. Some indoor leagues play on **turf**. Others play on concrete.

Goals are set up at each end of the field. A **crease** is marked on the field around each goal. Only the goalkeeper is allowed in the goal crease. The offensive/defensive zone is a large box around the crease.

The lacrosse goal has two 6-foot (1.8-m) poles attached at the top by a 6-foot (1.8-m) crossbar.

A centerline divides the field in half. Each end is marked with a centerline flag. The center of the field is marked with an "X." Flags also mark each corner of the playing field. They help players easily see the field's boundaries. The boundaries are called sidelines and endlines.

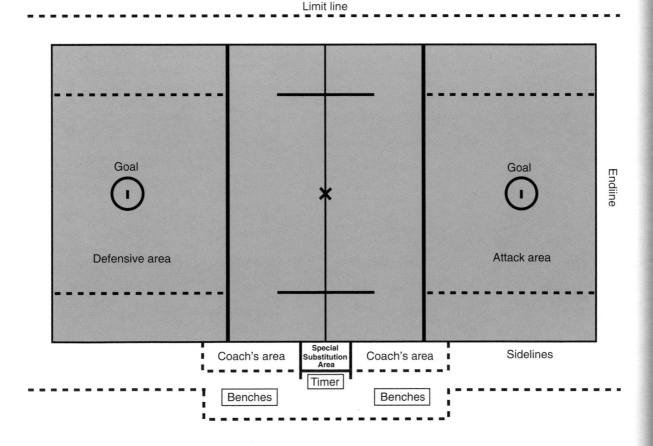

Limit line

Goal

Goal

Endline

Defensive area

Attack area

Coach's area

Special Substitution Area

Coach's area

Sidelines

Timer

Benches

Benches

Game Basics

College lacrosse games are 60 minutes long. High school games last 48 minutes. Games are divided into four quarters with a 10-minute rest period between halves. At the end of the game, the team with the most goals wins the game. If the score is tied at the end of the game, men's teams play 4-minute overtime periods to break the tie. The first team to score in an overtime period wins. Women's teams play two 3-minute overtime periods. The team that scores the most goals in overtime wins. If the game remains tied, they play until one team scores.

Players use lacrosse sticks to carry and pass the ball. The stick has a hook at the end that is strung with rawhide, **gut**, **nylon**, or linen cord to form a pocket that can hold the ball.

The goalkeeper's lacrosse stick has a larger head and pocket than the sticks used by other players.

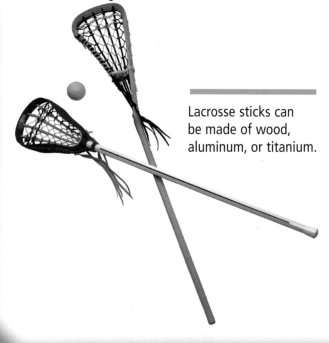

Lacrosse sticks can be made of wood, aluminum, or titanium.

All players can run with the ball. A player controls the ball by **cradling** it in the stick's head. Players pass the ball by flicking the stick forward. Players can pass the ball in any direction.

Players rarely attempt long passes because long passes often go out of bounds or are picked up by opponents. Usually, players run as far as they can before passing the ball to a teammate. Players make short, quick passes around the goal. They hope to move the defenders out of position and create gaps in front of the goal.

Physical contact is only allowed in men's lacrosse. Players use contact to stop their opponents and force them away from the goal. Players use their sticks to check, or hit the ballcarrier's stick to knock the ball from the pocket.

Play stops if the ball goes out of bounds or a **penalty** is called. When a player scores a goal, play also stops. Play does not stop if the ball hits the ground.

Aside from mouth guards, protective equipment is optional in women's lacrosse. Some players choose to wear gloves, nose guards, and helmets.

CHECK IT OUT

You can learn more lacrosse basics at

www.lacrosse.org/the_sport/ index.phtml

Positions and Plays

Box lacrosse teams have one goalkeeper and five runners. All runners play **offense** and **defense**. In women's lacrosse, each team has a goalkeeper, three offensive players, five midfielders, and three defensive players. Each men's field lacrosse team has a goalkeeper, three defensemen, three midfielders, and three attackers.

One of the midfielders is called the center. The center takes the **face-offs** that begin each period. The center and midfielders play offense and defense. They bring the ball forward to the attackers or help the defensemen guard the goal. Attackers usually have the best stick-handling skills. Midfielders are usually the fastest players on the team. Defenders are usually quick, strong players.

Offensive players must often dodge attacks from defensive players.

Play begins with a face-off at the center of the field. The official blows a whistle, and each center tries to gain control of the ball.

Each team must always have at least four players on the defensive side of the field and three on the offensive side. If a defensive player carries the ball over the centerline, another player must step back to the defensive side of the field. A team that has more than three players on the offensive side of the centerline is called offside by the referee.

If a player or team commits a penalty before or during a face-off, the opposing team gains possession of the ball.

CHECK IT OUT

Find out more about how lacrosse is played at

www.laxrules.com

Checks and Balances

In a men's lacrosse game, players can check with their bodies or sticks. Women are only allowed to hit the stick of a player carrying the ball.

In women's lacrosse a legal check is a tap on the opposing player's stick.

Male players can use their body to hit an opposing player carrying the ball or any opponent within 15 feet (5 m) of the ball. This is called a body check. Body checks must be made above the waist and from the front or side, never from behind. This rule reduces the chance of serious injury.

Players can use several methods to knock the ball from the pocket of the opponent's stick. They can hit their stick against their opponent's stick. They can poke their stick at a ballcarrier's hands. They can also slap the ballcarrier's hands.

In men's lacrosse, tackling opponents is common.

A penalty is called when a player commits the following fouls. The referee calls a personal foul when a player trips another player, makes an aggressive check, or makes an illegal body or stick check. A technical foul is called when a player pushes or holds an opponent, touches the ball with his or her hands, or goes offside. An expulsion foul is called if a player is too aggressive when hitting an opponent or uses abusive language with an official. A player who commits an expulsion foul is removed from the game.

Players who break the rules must serve a penalty for a certain amount of time. The player who received the penalty must leave the field. The team must play with one less player until the penalty is over or a goal is scored. The length of time that a player sits out varies according to the type of foul called.

Players often go to great lengths to prevent their opponents from gaining possession of the ball.

CHECK IT OUT

You can study lacrosse penalties in more detail by visiting
www.nll.com/article_250.shtml

Where the Action Is

Lacrosse is the fastest growing team sport in the United States. An estimated 125,000 U.S. children play lacrosse. There are more than 4,500 lacrosse programs in the United States. U.S. Lacrosse controls lacrosse across the country.

Thousands of students in U.S. high schools, colleges, and universities play lacrosse. College players often continue playing lacrosse in club **competition** after they graduate. The best college players sometimes join professional leagues. In North America, players can join the National Lacrosse League (NLL), which is box lacrosse, and Major League Lacrosse (MLL), which is field lacrosse.

Major League Lacrosse games are fast paced and exciting to watch.

Men's lacrosse was an Olympic sport in 1904 and 1908. Canada, England, and the United States participated. Canada won both gold medals. Lacrosse was an **exhibition** sport at the 1928, 1932, and 1948 Olympics. An exhibition tournament was held at the 1980 Olympic games. There are not enough national controlling groups to make lacrosse an official Olympic sport.

Women's sports experienced huge growth between 1975 and 2000. *Time* magazine featured women lacrosse players on the cover in 1978.

The first Men's World Lacrosse Championship was held in Toronto, Canada, in 1967. The International Lacrosse Federation has sponsored the championship since 1974, when the competition was held in Melbourne, Australia. It is held every 4 years.

In 1972, the International Federation of Women's Lacrosse Association (IFWLA) was established to control international women's competition. The association sponsors the IFWLA World Cup every 4 years. The first IFWLA World Cup was held in Nottingham, England, in 1982.

CHECK IT OUT

To read more about professional lacrosse, visit

www.plpa.com

Superstars of the Sport

Lacrosse has some well-known players. They entertain fans and break records.

JIM BROWN

HOMETOWN:
St. Simons Island, Georgia
POSITION:
Midfielder

Career Facts:

- Brown was born on February 17, 1936.
- Brown is considered one of the greatest players in college lacrosse history. He is also known as a great football running back.
- Syracuse University recruited Brown to play lacrosse.
- Brown was an **All-American** in 1956 and 1957.
- Brown was elected to the Lacrosse Hall of Fame in 1983.

PAUL GAIT

HOMETOWN:
Victoria, British Columbia, Canada
POSITION:
Midfielder

Career Facts:

- Paul Gait and his twin brother, Gary, were born on April 5, 1967.
- With his brother, Gary, Paul Gait helped lead Syracuse University to three straight National Collegiate Athletic Association (NCAA) lacrosse championships from 1988 to 1990.
- Paul Gait won the National Lacrosse League's Most Valuable Player award in 2002.
- Following a serious foot injury, Paul Gait retired after the 2002 season ended.

GARY GAIT

HOMETOWN:
Victoria, British Columbia, Canada
POSITION:
Midfielder

Career Facts:

- Gary Gait was a four-time All-American at Syracuse University.
- Gary Gait was NCAA National Player of the Year in 1988 and 1990.
- Gary Gait set two Syracuse University records with 192 career goals and 70 goals in one season. He also set the NCAA lacrosse tournament record for most goals, with 50 goals in 11 games.
- Gary Gait joined the National Lacrosse League in 1991. He has won the league's Most Valuable Player award six times.
- Gary Gait scored 61 goals in the 2002–2003 season, breaking his own record of 57 goals, set in 1988.

JEN ADAMS

HOMETOWN:
Brighton, Australia
POSITION:
Attacker

Career Facts:

- Adams is a three-time All-American. She won the NCAA National Player of the Year three times.
- Adams is the all-time leading points scorer in collegiate women's lacrosse.
- From 1998 to 2001, Adams scored 445 points, breaking a record that stood for more than 15 years.
- Adams is first in all-time assists (178), fourth in all-time goals (267), first and second in single-season points (148 in 2001 and 136 in 2000), and second and third in single-season assists (60 in 2001 and 55 in 2000).

Staying Healthy

Lacrosse is a physically demanding sport. Eating a healthy diet and practicing other types of exercise will help you enjoy lacrosse.

A healthy diet helps keep athletes strong. Eating foods from all of the food groups every day will keep a player's body in top condition. Grain products, fruits, and vegetables provide necessary vitamins, minerals, and fiber. Calcium keeps bones strong. Dairy products provide calcium. Meat provides protein to build muscles.

Eating five to nine servings of fruit and vegetables each day helps build strong bones and teeth.

CHECK IT OUT

Learn more about eating healthy by visiting

www.nalusda.gov/fnic

Drinking plenty of water before, during, and after lacrosse is important. Water keeps people's bodies cool. When lacrosse players sweat, they lose water. Drinking water replaces what is lost through sweat during a game.

Strong, flexible muscles are important for lacrosse players. Stretching keeps muscles flexible and prevents injuries. It is best to stretch during and after a **warm up**. Running in place for a few minutes or running a few laps warms muscles.

Lacrosse players often warm up together before games.

Playing lacrosse uses many muscles. Players must stretch their entire bodies to prevent injuries.

Lacrosse Brain Teasers

Test your knowledge of this fast-paced sport by trying to answer these lacrosse brain teasers!

Q Who invented the game of lacrosse?

A Native Americans invented the game of lacrosse.

Q What is the length of a lacrosse game?

A College lacrosse games are 60 minutes long. High school games are 48 minutes long.

Q What is another name for the lacrosse stick?

A The lacrosse stick is also known as the crosse.

Q Can lacrosse players touch the ball with their hands?

A Only the goalkeeper can touch the ball with his or her hands.

Q Is lacrosse an Olympic sport?

A No. There are not enough national controlling groups to make lacrosse an official Olympic sport. Lacrosse was an Olympic sport in 1904 and 1908.

Q What happens when a player commits a foul?

A The referee calls a penalty, and the player must leave the field. The amount of time that a player must sit out depends on the type of foul that has been called.

Glossary

All-American: selected and honored as a sport's best amateur player or athlete in the United States

bishops: people who oversee many churches

cleats: special athletic shoes with small spikes or tips on the bottom; they help players stop or turn quickly

competition: a contest between rivals

cradling: holding gently and carefully

crease: the 9-foot (2.7-meter) circle around the goal area

defense: the players trying to prevent the other team in a game from scoring

exhibition: a public performance

face-offs: putting the ball into play by dropping it between 2 players on opposing teams

gut: a strong cord made from the intestines of sheep

missionaries: people sent by religious groups to spread the religion in another country

nylon: a synthetic fabric

offense: the players trying to score in a game

penalty: punishment for breaking the rules

turf: artificial grass or field made of human-made material

warm up: gentle exercise to get a person's body ready for stretching and game play

Index